I Just Love to

FART

D1440429

COOK
BOOK

by Pazzin Gazz

I Just Love to Fart Cook Book

by Pazzin Gazz

© Copyright 2002
Lindsay Publications Inc
Bradley IL 60915

Printed and bound
in the United States of America.

ISBN 1-55918-275-X

2002

1   2   3   4   5   6   7   8   9   0

100% Restaurant Tested!
Proven at the Farts-R-Free Bar & Grill

The incredible recipes you find in this one-of-a-kind cookbook have been carefully reviewed by the waitressing staff of the Farts-R-Free Bar & Grill located in Phewmz, ND. These ladies can tell you without reservation that these recipes are among the most popular items on the menu (along with clothespins for the nose and replacement cartridges for all popular gas masks.) And, yes, the ladies DO wear their protective gear while waiting tables.

WARNING! WARNING!

Recipes contained in this cookbook could produce broken ribs and rolling pin contusions and could endanger the survival of your marriage! The publishers hereby disclaim all responsibility for explosions, failed relationships, asphyxiation, peeled paint, dead pets, unremovable stains, cracks in building foundations, lawsuits, and sundry other problems arising from the careless use of the information contained herein.

The Geneology of Bad Gas

CABBAGE FAMILY

You may enjoy researching past members of your family, but for those of us who derive intense pleasure from "cheesin' our pants," we're much more interested in the cabbage family. Knowing who's related to whom, will aid immensely in your cooking and farting adventures.

Cabbages–

Cauliflower – from the Middle East – great raw or steamed
Broccoli – green or purple – raw, or steamed & buttered
Kale – great Mediterranean green leaves, best steamed & buttered
Brussels Sprouts – miniature heads of cabbage
Green Cabbage – cheap & deadly – great with Corned Beef
Bok Choy – long stalks & small leaves – Chinese stir-fried
Chinese Cabbage – elongated version of green cabbage
Red Cabbage – green cabbage with an identity problem
Kohlrabi – more like a cross between a cabbage and a carrot

COLON CRAMPIN' COLE SLAW

Gute ol' cole slaw: the Kaiser's cabbage salad. Just a bit of this will introduce your intestinal plumbing to new pleasures that simply cannot be described, only experienced.

cabbage	about half a head
carrots	a couple
celery	a stalk or two
mayonnaise	4 tablespoons or more
vinegar, malt or red wine	a couple of tablespoons
sugar	a tablespoon or so
salt & pepper	to taste

This powerful anal explosive is so easy to mix up. And really good, too! Make it the way you like it.

Shred the cabbage. A knife will do, but a coarse slicing blade on a food processor makes quick work of it. Chop, grind, or shred the carrots. Slice the celery very thin.

The dressing has to be made to your specs. A little experience will show you what's needed.

Put the mayonnaise in a covered jar. Add the vinegar, sugar, salt and pepper, and shake. Stick your finger, toe or other portion of your anatomy into the mix and taste it.

Too tart? Add sugar. Not tart enough? Add a dash of vinegar. Too powerful in flavor? Add more mayonnaise. Too thick? Add a dash of milk. Experiment until you get the dressing the way you like it and toss it over the vegetables. Not enough to cover all the cabbage the way you like it? Then make some more! Tough, huh?

You can mix up a bushel basket of this stuff for pennies. It has great nutritional value and is more fun than a tour of the local sewage treatment plant. But your wife and/or girlfriend won't think so in a couple of hours...

Gazzmayne's Big Blast!

Georgie Gazzmayne, a local farmer, back about 1912 was known throughout the area as a cabbage farmer without equal. His cabbages were the largest, sweetest, and most prolific gas producers the country had ever seen. Vegetable dealers through the country offered premiums to obtain some of his cabbage.

Naturally ol' Gazzmayne became quite affluent, and decided to buy himself a brand new four-cylinder Blappmobile. Georgie, of course, ate enormous amounts of his own cabbage, and was terminally afflicted by what doctors called *extremus fartitis*. And that was his downfall.

While polishing up his new automobile in his closed garage, Georgie had to let rip a cabbage-induced anal seizure which filled the garage with a cloud of extremely explosive gas. When the cloud reached the kerosene lamp, the gas exploded, lifted the garage fifty feet straight into the air which then fell straight down on Gazzmayne and his car, killing him instantly.

R.I.P.

GARBAGE DUMP CABBAGE

You never outgrow your need for cabbage. It will put hair on your chest. It will even put hair on your tongue! And will it ever add thrust to your afterburner!

cabbage, shredded	five or six cups
butter or olive oil	three or four tablespoons
whipping cream	about 1/2 a cup
salt & pepper	to taste

After a hard day of digging through the land fill looking for something to sell on my favorite internet auction site at a price a hundred times greater than even my retarded sister would pay, I chow down on cabbage. Could there be anything better?

Chop that cabbage up into pieces small enough to fit into your mouth. (I do assume that you intend to pack it into your mouth.) Put it into a fry pan with a tight cover and saute in the butter for about ten minutes over low heat. It would be wise to stir once or twice.

Now comes the complicated part. Dump in the cream, salt & pepper, and saute about another five minutes. Try not to overcook the cabbage or it will get soggy. About like your brain after a tough day at the dump.

Serve with bratwurst quickly cooked over a fire of scrap wood burning in a old fifty-five gallon drum. Serve with a bottle wine on sale from the local discount liquor store – and remember: it's on sale because no one in their right mind would buy it at even a discount price.

Bon appetite. For you hicks, that's French for "watch out for the bones."

Great Stinking Times! Always! At the

FARTS-R-FREE BAR & GRILL

Great food, fun times!

When in Phewmz, please visit us! Enjoy the latest gas inducing cuisine prepared by world-famous Chef, Wiffa la Pew. Join in the festivities.

And be sure to leave your aromatic calling card!

Open any day of the year the Environmental Protection Agency permits. From 11 am until the neighbors complain!

CHINESE PICKLED CABBAGE

Call it what you want. To us at the Farts-R-Free Bar & Grill, we know it as cooked Chinese coleslaw. It's potent, and popular with our pants-destroying customers...

```
cabbage (white preferred, green okay) .. a couple of pounds
soy sauce (the richer, the better) ...... about two tablespoons
brown sugar ........................................... two tablespoons
vinegar (wine, cider or malt) .......... about three tablespoons
salt ....................................................... about a teaspoon
oil (peanut, not 10W-30) .................................... not much
```

Cut the tender innards of the cabbage roughly into cubes. The tough core and coarse outer leaves you can feed to the pigs or your in-laws (if there's a difference.)

Put a couple of tablespoons of oil in a wok and stir fry the cabbage until it becomes translucent, but not so long that it gets limp. Drain and put in a bowl.

Mix the soy sauce, brown sugar, vinegar, salt, and another tablespoon of oil, and dump into the wok. Heat long enough to dissolve all of the sugar and then pour over the cabbage.

I suppose you can eat it immediately, but it will taste far better if you let it sit in the 'fridge for several hours or overnight.

The Real Phineas Fogg

For many years, rumors circulated asserting that the "Around the World in Eighty Days" character, Phineas Fogg, was based on the notorious Wall Street trader, Peter "Pants Eater" Pew, who once tried to the corner the market in kidney beans. (And from the smell that followed him around, you'd swear he had!)

TRADITIONAL CABBAGE ROLLS

Rather than roll the leaves up and smoke them like we used to do in the 60's, we now roll them up around nasty fillings, eat them, and let our butt's smoke!

```
cabbage ................................... a medium head
butter .................................................. 2 tbl
tomato juice ........................... a cup or more
salt & pepper ............................... to taste
cooked rice................................ about 2 cups
onion, chopped .......................... one medium
butter ............................... half a stick or more
```

Chop the cabbage in half and carefully remove the core and worst outer leaves. You want only the best outer leaves. Put the halves in a pan and cover with boiling water (add salt if you wish), and let sit until the leaves are pliable and can be rolled around the filling.

Lay out a couple of leaves, put a couple of spoonfuls of rice filling made from the rice, onion and butter, and roll up. Make the whole thing stay together by stabbing it with a toothpick or two. Pour a little melted butter and/or tomato juice over the rolls, and bake in a covered dish for one to two hours.

If the leaves are hard to roll, use a potato peeler to shave off the thick center veins of the leaves. Put any remaining butter and tomato juice in the bottom of the dish to help cooking. Consider wrapping bacon around the rolled up cabbage leaves for extra flavor.

Best of all, forget the rice filling and fill those mothers with refried beans, and lots of 'em. Do that, you'll be talkin' through yer butt, for hours...

Better yet, fill the cabbage leaves with refried beans mixed with pea gravel. Feed them to your bitchy Aunt Claude and turn her into a human shot gun!

The Quickest Way to A Man's Heart

It has always been said that the quickest way to a man's heart is through his stomach. But the important anatomy lies on the far side of the stomach: the colon.

A man's appetite for sex diminishes as he ages, but a real man never outgrows his love for passing gas.

A woman who lovingly feeds a man's colon knowing that doing so will cause cracked china, tarnished silver, discolored wallpaper, and other problems is a rare find – a woman to be treasured!

"RED EYE" CABBAGE CARNAGE

This secret weapon was used in Viet Nam and did far more damage than B-52s and agent orange. And, of course, any Jar Head will tell "I just love the smell of flatus in the morning..."

red cabbage .... one head (bones removed)
apples, sour, red prefereably .... a fine pair
salt .... 2 tsp (more if you can stand it)
cider vinegar .... 1/2 cup
sugar .... 1/2 cup
flour to thicken .... a tablespoon or so

Remove the nasty outer leaves of the cabbage and shred whatever might left over. Hint: there should be something left over. Core the apples, and cut into thin slices.

Now, this is the complicated part. Throw everything in a pan along with about 1/2 a cup of water, cover, and cook for 20 to 30 minutes. An expert cook (which you can't possibly be if you're reading this!) might stir cabbage carnage occasionally.

When cooked, dissolve the flour in a little cold water, stir in and cook a minute or so until the sauce thickens.

If you have a strong enough stomach, fill a bunch of soup bowls and serve immediately. If you aren't that sadistic, feed it to your dog, and cover every inch of the floor with a thick layer of newspapers for the indescribable mess that you know will soon be arriving!

When Peter Pan opened in the West End theater district of London more than a century ago, the lead role was played by Angela Nozzelbut, who was chosen for her ability to fly across the stage without wires. Unfortunately, the first ten rows of theater seats could never be sold, and the theater was forced to replace her with another actress possessing more mainstream talents.

FRIED CABBAGE FROM THE SEWERS OF HADES...

If you're Irish, you don't need this recipe. A corned-beef brisket is all you need. For the rest of us intent on driving way relatives and attracting hoards of dung-beetles, this will get us talkin' through our butts.

```
cabbage ................................. they come in heads, get one
bacon, blubbery salt pork ........................ 1/2 pound (8 oz)
onions ................................................ 1, preferably more
tomatoes .......... 3 or 4 large fresh ones, or a couple of cans
sugar .......................................... 1-2 teaspoons or to taste
hot pepper (cayenne, flakes, Chipotle) ................... to taste,
                                                add a little at a time
                                                and sample it
```

Put the bacon or salt pork in a pot, and slowly cook it until the fat starts to render out. Dump in cabbage that you've chopped into pieces or into strands. Fry until the cabbage is limp and starts to brown a little. Dump in your chopped up tomatoes or the canned variety. Cook this for 30 minutes or until the tomatoes lose their shape, and the goop thickens up like spaghetti sauce. Taste it. Add a small amount of sugar to neutralize some of the acid from the tomatoe, if you like. Spice it up with hot pepper as well as the usual salt and fresh-ground black pepper. My sister-in-law, Rufus, says down south people call this a stew and serve it on rice. Up here in the North where people take great pride in being able to fart in time to the national anthem at ball games, we usually serve it on pasta. Me? I serve it on a shingle.

Cracks in the Foundation

Mysterious cracks appeared in the stone foundation of the Farts-R-Free Bar & Grill 'long about 1951. The owner hired Dr. Bituminous Buttfogg of Pustule University (ol' P.U.) to study the problem. Ol' Doc Buttfogg oversaw the sewer lab at the university so he was no rocket scientist. But he didn't need to be. One small wiff of the odor emanating from the dining room filled with customers and their singing sphincters, and Doc knew that the foundation mortar was being attacked by bad gas.

Seen here is the instrument he devised to measure foundation fractures from flatulence. It's a modified seismograph, but it no longer uses the Richter scale. No, Doc devised what he called the 1-to-10 Sphincter Scale. To this day when a Bar & Grill customer rips one, waitresses hold up large scoring cards: 9.8, 9.9, 9.6, and 9.9, and once a month someone is awarded a gold medal for their performance.

SAUERKRAUT & NECK BONES

Cabbage is the elixir of life to a fart-aholic. But sauerkraut (rotten cabbage) smells bad before you get into your mouth!
What happens to it in your gut, and what it does to your anal sphincter is pure magic!

```
sauerkraut ................................. as much as you can stand
neckbones ............................... lots, they're cheap,
                                          flavorful but little meat
salt, sugar, plaster of paris ....... try anything to improve the
                                          flavor, but I think you're
                                          wasting your time!
```

Another tough dish. A no brainer. Put the sauerkraut in a pot. Add salt, pepper, and maybe a hit of sugar to improve it. Throw in the bones and simmer for as long as you can stand the stench. Then simply serve it in your favorite trough. If you're daring you can add at the last minute, a cup of vodka, a dead squirrel, a pair of very old gym socks, or the tee-shirt stolen from that wino who sleeps under the bridge. Just about anything will improve the flavor.

Sure, this stuff ain't the most tasty dish in my opinion, but when you combine this toxic waste with bean mush, celery sticks, pecans and hazel nuts, you're gonna be able to knock a crow off a fence post at a hundred yards with a single blast from your anal cannon.

The Surgeon General Has Found that Farting in a Zoo Can Be Dangerous to Your Health!

If you offend some smelly wild beast with your smelly wild vapors the beasts might take matters into their own teeth! You have been warned.

SWAMP GAS STEW A LA STINK...

Another great one dish meal, guaranteed to stick to your ribs and perhaps your underwear as well.

```
stew meat ................................................ about a pound
yellow onion ....................................................... medium
cabbage, chopped ................. a cup or two (more is better)
celery, chopped ............................................ half to full cup
beans ...................... 16 oz can, or a cup or two of your own
tomatoes .................. two chopped, or a can from the store
salt & pepper ...................................... to taste (what else?)
```

Correct posture for performing the "silent but deadly" diversionary tactic.

Brown the meat over high heat in a little vegetable oil. Reduce the heat, and fry the onion, cabbage and celery until soft, translucent, and kind of yellowish (kind of like your mother-in-law's complexion). Add a cup or so of water and simmer for 10 or 15 minutes until a lot of the water has boiled away. Put in the rest of the ingredients and simmer another 10 to 15 minutes. This is another of them there fixin's that gotta be served on a shingle. Ida know you's guests is gonna think you's outta yer haid. (But you'll be enshrined in the Flatulence Hall of Fame. So let 'em think anything they want.)

Essence of Fart Oil

In the fall of 1929, Herbert "The Load" Boopster developed a process to extract the gas-forming chemicals found in cabbage and beans and condense them into a highly-concentrated tasteless liquid, he called "essence of fart oil."

Working with Elliot Ness in Chicago, Boopster, posing as an ace brewmaster from the old country, infiltrated the Capone breweries throughout the Chicago area. Unknown to the gangsters, Boopster spiked all outgoing beer and spirits with his fart oil. Within days, Ness and the Untouchables were able to locate every speakeasy in town by the smell leaking out into the streets.

By the time Ness and his crew had raided every speak in the city, their noses had been irreversibly burned by the unspeakable tavern gas. All lost their sense of smell. Shortly thereafter, Untouchables became known as the Unsmellables.

BIOGAS SOUP

In some poor countries, manure is put in big tanks to ferment into methane gas to be used in electrical generators and gas stoves. With this basic vegetable soup recipe, YOU become the big tank! But DON'T hook your butt up to your gas stove. It might be the last thing you ever do!

```
yellow onion ................................................ one medium
garlic ..................................... as much as you dare, minced
chicken broth ..... you can use canned, better if you make it
cabbage ................... 1/4 to 1/2 head chopped or shredded
celery.............................. 4-6 ribs chopped, more is better!
green beans ...... a couple of cups, chopped, more is better!
pieces of chicken................................. a couple of breasts
                                    or four thighs, just the meat
potatoes ....... a couple of handfuls of small peeled potatoes
```

Slowly cook the onion and garlic in a bit of olive oil in the bottom of pan until soft and translucent. Add the broth, and bring up the heat. Put in the vegetables and meat and simmer for 20-30 minutes. Add salt and pepper to taste.

This is a general recipe open to wide variation. You can use just about any vegetables, but cabbage, celery, and beans are best if you intend to become a professional competition anal orator. You can add fresh herbs and spices, tomatoes, make it with fish, ham, and just about any mold-free thing you find hiding in the bottom of the refrigerator. Try adding the juice of a lemon just before serving. I used Tangaray Gin once, but it didn't taste so hot. But all my guests were so drunk they didn't care. They had disastrous hangovers the next day, and every butt blast made their head ring with excruciating pain, so I don't recommend gin.

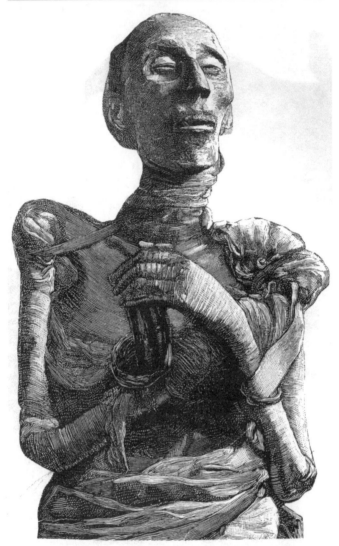

Ancient Egyptian Pharoh,

King Phartten-runn, was the only Pharoh who smelled better dead than he did alive!

CABBAGE & BLUBBER

This recipe is as old as America. I am absolutely convinced that the British forced the American colonists to leave Britain because they polluted the air so badly. And that was in a time when the air was filled with coal smoke, horse manure, and the odor of unwashed bodies!

cabbage .... a couple of medium sized heads
salt pork .... 1/2 pound (8 oz) or more
onions, standard old yellow .... one or two
salt, pepper, toilet bowl cleaner, etc .... to taste
(if you have any left)

I can't believe early Americans ate this stuff! They must have been desperate. Salt pork. There ain't no pork to it. Just fat. Lots of fat and salt (just what we want.) Chop the salt pork into small pieces. Put the pork in a cast iron skillet (but I like to use a cast iron Dutch oven.) Cook the salt pork slowly to render down some of the fat into a liquid on the bottom of the pan in which you can fry the cabbage and onion. Cook everything over medium heat until the onion is translucent and the cabbage is wilted. Season and serve.

Whatcha gotta do, is make this up for the Sunday evening meal. Long about Monday night, you sit down with a case of cheap beer and a bushel basket of popcorn and/or chips to watch Monday night football. Just as the ball is kicked off, you'll feel your colon come to life, and before long you'll be talking through your butt to the officials about that last bad call. What joy! Football, beer, and gas!

The Geneology of Bad Gas
SEED FAMILY

You may enjoy researching past members of your family, but for those of us who derive intense pleasure from "airing out the back porch," we're much more interested in the bean family. Knowing who's related to whom, will aid immensely in your cooking and farting adventures.

Beans—

Navy – small round white bean (Boston baked Beans)
Mung – from India & China – use as bean sprouts
Great Northern – white, large, flat – stews & casseroles
Black – South American – served with meat, sometimes fried
Kidney – red, kidney shaped (what else?) – great for chili
Lima – discovered in South America, large, white, flat
Butter – another name for Lima
Aduki – Oriental, small red or black – sweet, strong flavor
Soy – small, circular, yellowish – soy sauce, tofu, noodles, etc
Chinese – small, black – usually fermented!! cooked with meat
Pinto – small, tan with brown spots – general purpose

Lentils—

Green – small, circular, & green – common, tasty
Yellow – small, circular & yellow (surprise!), common in Asia
Flageolet – green, French – delicate taste great in salads

Nuts—

Almonds, cashews, walnuts, pecans, Brazil, Hazelnut, Macadamia, Chestnuts, and many more that you've already probably tried. Eat enough nuts, and you'll discover a whole new way to express yourself.

VEGETARIAN GRENADES

(Who would have thought Mother Nature could have been so cruel...)

beans, soaked (in water, not vodka) .... 4 cups
bacon .... 1/2 pound (or more)
onion, finely chopped .... 2 medium or 1 large
pepper, preferably fresh ground .... 1/4 tsp (or more)
salt (not salt peter) .... 2 tsp
water (boring but useful) .... enough to cover the beans

Soak the beans overnight in water. Then pick out the deformed beans and throw them away (or force feed them to your bitchy Aunt Betty.) Pitch the beans, salt, pepper, bacon and onion into a large pot. I like to slowly cook bacon down to remove fat, and then use only the crisp, meaty bacon that remains. Cover this revolting concoction with water (unless you happen to prefer Chardonnay.) Bring to boil, reduce heat, and simmer for a couple of hours, or how ever long it takes to make them palatable (in other words, an eternity.) Once soft enough to chew with your dentures removed, serve immediately – before your guests understand exactly how you intend to torture them. (Alternative: puree in a blender and administer intravenously or load into a turkey baster and administer anally. No.... they just might LIKE that...)

Beanology
Beans of very deadly character!

Common Pinto bean. No doubt named after an automobile that when hit in the rear end had a nasty habit of surprising everyone with its unstable gas tank. Common, inexpensive. A great way to refill your highly unstable intestinal gas tank.

Expolsivus Flattus Extremus, also known as the Asian spotted detonator bean. Very dangerous. Illegal! Now banned in almost every country. So deadly that it was once feared even more than small pox and the Black Death.

    If you convert your kitchen into a biohazard containment laboratory (which it probably already is), you may want to try to have a supply smuggled in. Reportedly the only place in the world where the bean is still cultivated is the small country of Hufartistan, once part of the Soviet Union. Sometimes offered for sale in the bazaars of

Common Red bean. Common in availability. Common in price. But anything but common in producing fuel for your anal cannon. You get lots of gas for a dollar's worth of beans, and they're easy to cook as well.

Stinqonia. Careful! If you get caught possessing such beans, penalties are severe for you and the people who have to smell you!

THE ADMIRAL'S BEANS & RICE

This is NOT served to sailors stationed on submarines. No submariner should have to fear depth charges coming from within the sub itself!

```
dried beans, red will do ............................ about a pound
yellow onion, chopped ................................. about a cup
scallions (known as green onions among rednecks) ..... a few
chopped celery ............................... 1/2 cup or so
chopped green peppers ............................... 1/2 cup or so
sausage, Polish, Italian, your choice ...... a couple of pounds
tomatoes (optional) ...... a can from the grocery storeminced
garlic ................................. three cloves or more
fresh minced parsley .................................... lots
chili powder ................................. 1 teaspoon
```

Soak the beans overnight to soften. They're just too hard on the teeth otherwise. Saute the onion, garlic, celery and peppers in a little oil for 15-20 minutes, and dump into a large pan with the beans. Add at least four cups of water. Cut the sausage into bite-size pieces and add along with all the remaining ingredients.

Cover the pot and bring to a boil. Then turn the heat down and cook very slowly for a couple of hours. Check frequently as cooking progresses. If the water is completely absorbed, add more to prevent burning. But don't add so much that the beans can't absorb it. You can always remove a small amount of cook beans at the end, run them through a blender to create a paste and then add back to the pot to make a kind of bean sauce or gravy. Serve this mess over rice. Be sure to use old newspapers as a table cloth to add a high class touch your dinner party.

Sound really bad doesn't it? And it makes really bad sounds, too!

"BUTT BUSTIN'" BEAN SOUP

(Supposedly Mexican in origin. But the Mexicans I know are such nice people, I would never want to blame something this bad on them!)

Navy Beans (dry - Army beans won't do) .... 1 Cup
water (clean and cold) .... 6 Cups
oil (vegetable NOT 10W-40) .... 1/4 cup more or less
garlic, minced .... 2 cloves or more
onion, chopped .... 1/3 cup or more
parsley, fresh chopped .... 2 tbl
celery, chopped .... 2 cups
cabbage, chopped or shredded .... 1 cups
salt .... 1/4 cup (or less)
pepper, fresh ground if possible .... 1/4 tsp
tomatoes, canned .... 12-16 oz
noodles or favorite pasta .... 2 cups cooked

Wash the beans. Put them in a large pot with the water and bring to a boil. Reduce the heat and simmer until tender (a couple of hours is not unusual.) In another pot or large fry pan saute the garlic, onion, parsley, celery and cabbage in the oil until slightly browned (about 20 minutes.) You can brown them instantly with an oxyacetylene torch, but that will ruin the flavor (and the kitchen.) Throw this mess into the beans. Add the salt, pepper, tomatoes, and anything else that sounds interesting and cook it for another half hour or so. You can then pour this revolting looking dish over your favorite pasta (a preferably gas-generating variety) or throw the cooked pasta right into the bean soup. Serves about a dozen people, but you might want to eat the whole thing yerself and generate enough gas to kill a dozen people!

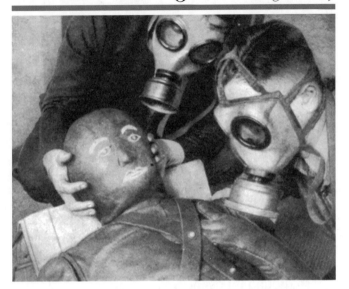

Crash Test Dummy "Killed" by Flatulence!

Gas mask testing at the Farts-R-Free Bar & Grill was conducted by the United States Army Flatulence Countermeasures Laboratory from 1917 until 1948. Tests were discontinued when their crash test dummy was accidentally destroyed during one particularly busy lunch hour when 418 construction workers demanded more of the toxic bean soup they had been served the day before.

When the local fire marshal discovered that the crash test dummy had "died", an ordnance was enacted requiring the Bar & Grill to use fire department smoke ejectors whenever more than 215 people were inside the notoriously smelly restaurant. Since then, downtown Phewmz has been rat-free and roach-free, but has been overrun by Saharan dung beetles attracted by the smell!

SUCCOTRASH

This stuff is bland going down, but not coming out. Suck a pile of this trash and enjoy!

```
soaked beans (lima are good) ................. two cups or more
corn out of the can, or cut off the cob ........ about two cups
whipping cream .......................................... about 1/2 cup
butter or olive oil ................................. about a tablespoon
salt, pepper, and Portland cement ......................... to taste
```

Throw everything a pan and heat over medium heat for 10 to 20 minutes. Taste every so often. If you can finally tolerate it, then eat it.

Cooking it is easy. Eating it is the tough part. Letting the world understand with their noses exactly what you've been through should be an exciting new experience for you, and an act of terrorism for them!

Army cook, Maak M. Pewq, was court marshalled in 1919 for serving World War I troops "succotrash" while simultaneously receiving a Purple Heart for enduring the results of his mistake.

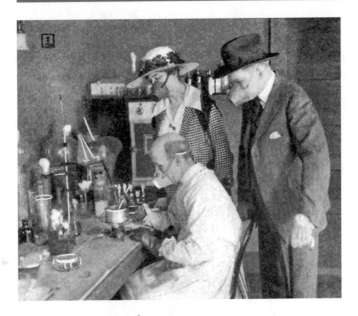

Procto's Pinto Bean

In the 1920's, Americans saw patenting an invention as the road to wealth. Wanting to claim their share of the riches, Mr. and Mrs. Paynefell Procto and Grandad Procto were able to crossbreed an especially virulent pinto bean so incredibly foul that it was almost impossible to get close enough to it to cook it. And after it was cooked and eaten, well... that's a story in unsurpassed heroism.

As a test, Grandad ingested a full one-pound (dry weight) of the bean they named *anus vaporous prolifigus*, swelled to almost half the size of the Hindenberg, was struck by lightning, and crashed and burned at Lakehurst NJ in 1931. Unfortunately, no newsreel cameras nor crying commentators were on hand to document the calamity.

Shortly thereafter, the seed stock was confiscated by the newly-formed FBI, declared a danger to society, and destroyed.

BASIC FLATULENCE FUEL

THE single most important food group among those in training to compete in the World Fart Off competition held each year in Braaaap, Slovakia.

beans (Lima, Navy, etc) .... 1 pound (about 2 cups dry)
salt pork, ham hock, road kill, sumthin' .... 1/2 pound minimum
onion, yellow .... 1 large

You can soak the beans overnight before cooking, but it's not necessary. Just throw the beans into a pot with a couple of quarts of water, and the meat you're going to use for flavoring and bring to boil. Simmer for 2 to 3 hours until you can mash the beans down into a paste. I understand the Cajuns down in the bayous like to spice up this GAStronomical essential with a cup or two of chopped green onions and sometimes parsley. Other people spike this goop with a bit of sugar, a dash of vinegar, and sometimes nutmeg.

A clothespin on the nose is certainly cheaper than a gas mask and a supply of charcoal filters. But a clothespin forces you to breathe through your mouth. Do you really want to abuse your tastebuds in that way?

Frances Willard Founded the WCTU

We all know that Frances Willard founded the Women's Christian Temperance Union to fight the ill effects stemming from the consumption of alcoholic beverages. But few people realize that her sister "Weird Wanda" founded the WMEFB: Women's Movement to End Farting in Bed.

Weird Wanda's rolling pin and frying pin had only a momentary effect on her wimpy husband's sheet raising behavior. Her Movement was ineffective. But his movements were legendary.

Wanda and other women weary from attempting to keep sheet and blankets on the bed while their oblivious husbands passed gas wished their husbands would start snoring instead. And wish is about all they could do.

HOWITZER'S BEAN SALAD

Most people associate the name Howitzer with a high-trajectory cannon. Not here. This is Herman Howitzer's way of achieving high muzzle velocity.

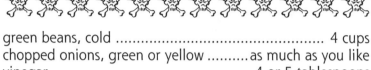

green beans, cold	4 cups
chopped onions, green or yellow	as much as you like
vinegar	4 or 5 tablespoons
sugar	a tablespoon or more (to taste)
sour cream	half a cup or more
salt, pepper, PCBs, dioxin	to taste

Cook the beans, and let them cool. After all, this IS a salad. I like to steam fresh green beans for maximum flavor. Consider cutting them across or lengthways to make them easier to stuff into your mouth.

Mix the beans with the onion. Put the vinegar, sour creams, salt, pepper and other toxins in a small container, and shake to mix. Stick your cleanest finger (if any are at all clean) into the sauce and taste it. Add more ingredients until it tastes the way you like it, or until you run out of ingredients or fingers. But I suppose you could use your toes, or someone else's fingers.

Pour the sauce over the beans and scarf those suckers down.

Idea: set a timer and see how long it takes before you're able to drop your pants and recite the Gettysburg address.

General Grant once admitted the only reason the North won the Civil War was because the Southern farmers grew cotton and the Northern farmers grew beans and cabbage.

Virulent Vapor Analyzer

In the years following World War I, Professor Waybad Zmell of Pustule University (ol' P.U.), was commissioned by the U.S. Army to develop a way to measure the toxicity of enemy military poison gas. Before the device could be perfected however, the Geneva convention outlawed the use of such gas.

Development continued when a top General pointed out that more soldiers were overcome by the indescribable fog emanating from Army latrines than from any foreign power. Professor Zmell's electronic nose was used to reduce Army outhouse casualties, and then leased to a large corporation for commercial development.

Today, one of the last remaining analyzers of its kind has been used to test the recipes in this book. Only the worst have been printed here. Soldiers can thank the professor for his contributions to army life, but if you stand down wind from another owner of this cookbook, you just may want to curse the memory of Professor Zmell.

RECTAL FIRE BEAN LOAF

I got this recipe from my Aunt Kooter just after she got out of prison. She only did four years of her thirty year sentence, so it must have been because she was put in charge of the prison kitchen. Her cooking was considered cruel and unusual punishment.

beans, kidney, white, your choice .... 2 cups
bread crumbs .... at least 3 cups, probably more
cheddar cheese, grated .... at least a couple of cups
onion .... somewhat less than a cup
oil, vegetable .... about 1/2 cup
egg .... 1 should do it
salt .... 1 tsp
pepper, fresh ground .... lots

This is just meat loaf but without the meat. Soak the beans overnight, and simmer the next day until quite tender. Let 'em cool, and them mash them into a paste. Add the oil which replaces the fat usually found in meat. Mix in the onion, cheese, salt and pepper. Next add the egg (the glue), and mix the whole repulsive mess up with your hands. Once thoroughly combined, add in breadcrumbs until this goop begins to dry up and get stiff.

Then you pack this into a loaf pan that you've greased up (to prevent sticking) and bake at 350°F for 60 to 90 minutes.

You can slice the loaf up and make sandwiches. But this is another one of those dishes I prefer to serve on shingles. Try fresh-ground Parmesan instead of cheddar. And try adding a teaspoon or so of fennel seed. It's hard to believe that just a couple slices of this will having you cheesin' your pants for days!

Farts-R-Free
—BAR & GRILL—

★ ★ ★ ★

What the Critics Are Saying!

"The Farts-R-Free Bar & Grill is a truly gastronomical experience that will bring tears to your eyes, and pain to your nostrils. The food is good, too." –editor, MANURE SPREADERS GAZETTE

"Bean cuisine at it's best! Such ambience! Just bring a megaphone so you can make yourself heard over the unimaginable background noise! Reservations and a gas mask are recommended" –restaurant editor, MALIGNANT MIST MAGAZINE

"An essential part of good health. Truly great, low cholesterol, high gas foods that will cleanse your intestines, fumigate for termites, and drive away obnoxious in-laws. A magical anal experience. Four stars!" –THE GAStronomical HEALTH PERFECTIONIST

SPHINCTER STRETCHER CASSEROLE

Forget the tuna! Forget the noodles! If you want to dilate your most important bodily orifice to a new level of ecstasy, build your next casserole with beans!

```
bacon ............................................ about four slices cut up
store-bought chili sauce ................................... about a cup
cooked kidney beans ......................................... 4 to 5 cups
onion, chopped .......................... one small one oughta do
honey ................................................................ 1/3 cup
mustard, dry (again NOT mustard gas) .......... 1 tsp or more
salt & pepper ....................................................... to taste
```

Cook the bacon slowly in a fry pan to render out the fat. When the bacon starts to get crisp, remove it, leaving the drippings behind. Throw the chopped onion into the bacon fat and cook until softened, about 10 minutes. Turn off the heat and let cool down a bit.

Dump the onion and the drippings (and the pan, too, if you like the taste of metal) into a casserole dish. Add everything else, including the cooked bacon. Stir it all up with a toilet bowl brush, and cover. Put it into a preheated 400° oven about half an hour until it's bubbling like a hot sulfur spring in Hades.

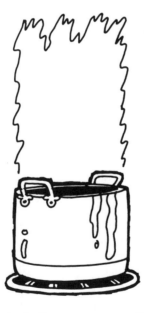

Serves four to six normal people, but since you're not normal, eat it all yourself. A spoon might be too small. Try a snow shovel. In a matter of just hours, you'll sound like a steam calliope on steroids!

First Stink Ejector

In 1937 rotting corpses stolen from a local undertaking parlor were hidden under the tables at the Farts-R-Free Bar & Grill in attempt to freshen the air. When that didn't work, "Flush-It-Again" Norton, the head cook and part-time sewer cleaner, mounted a 1924 Model T engine on a four legged stand. A propeller from a 1918 Curtiss Jenny was mounted on the transmission shaft to create a gigantic fan.

Unfortunately, the ejector didn't work very well. It was so powerful that it blew the tables, chairs, silverware, two waitresses, and an enormous cloud of stink across the street into the X-rated movie theater. Due to the heavy breathing going on in the theater, eighteen perverts, nine deviates, and an insurance salesman were instantaneously overcome by the smell.

The fan did little to alleviate the stink left behind by bean-eating, cabbage-gorging restaurant customers. It just wasn't powerful enough.

SADDAM'S KILLER CUCUMBERS!

Fry up come cucumbers as a side dish to beans, and you'll everyone on your side of town will know what you've been up to! This stuff will create endless clouds of toxic butt fumes. You'll knock crop-dusters outta the sky!

cucumbers .... the more, the better

flour, bread crumbs,crushed
cornflakes, cornmeal .... 2 cups at least,
                                      more may be needed

vegetable oil (with a little bacon fat mixed in)......... enough
                            to cover the cucumbers for frying

salt, pepper, quick-lime, other seasoning .... as needed

It don't get no easier than this, jack! Slice the cucumbers lengthwise, in half or maybe even in quarters. You put the bread crumbs, flour, corn meal or whatever combination you like into a plastic bag, brown paper bag, or your cross-dressing Uncle Rudolph's favorite purse. You put a few slices in the bag, shake it carefully to coat the cucumbers. Next, you fry the slices in

hot oil until they're golden brown, or until the kitchen catches fire and you have to run for your life! You can season the slices before you coat them or after, or add the seasonings to the bag of crud. After you take these deadly gas generators out of the oil, drain them on something absorbent and elegant like the obituary page from the local newspaper.

Six Warning Signs
that He's Going to "Bust the Big One!"

1. Belly distended.
2. Legs apart.
3. Eyes rolled back in pain and/or ecstasy.
4. Newspaper positioned to deflect away the toxic cloud.
5. One last gasp before holding the breath.
6. Nail studded stick in hat to fend off complainers should anyone survive the blast.

BASIC BAD BUTTERED BROCCOLI

Don't try this dish if you plan to burgle someone's home. No matter how dark it may be, everyone in the neighborhood will know by the sound and the smell that you're nearby!

broccoli, bright green and fresh	lots
water, preferably clean	as much as it takes
salt	enough
vinegar	a small amount
butter	plenty, to kill the taste

Traditionally, the broccoli is soaked in salt water to which a little vinegar has been added. This usually drives out any bugs that might be hiding in the buds. But our family was so poor that we ate the broccoli with bugs as a way to add a little protein to our diet! If your broccoli don't got no bugs, add some. Try some roaches, that is, cockroaches. You know. Those critters growing by the millions under the sink.

Drain and rinse the broccoli, and put in a large pot. Covered with mildly salted water. How much salt to add? Just taste the water, and add salt until you get it where you like it.

Boil the broccoli about 20 to 30 minutes until the thick stems are tender enough to get a fork into. Melt a little butter over the hot broccoli and serve.

Most people think that broccoli stinks while it's cooking. Some of us think it smells great! Most people will find out how bad it truly smells once it goes through your digestive system!

43

Canaries Are Not Used

For centuries coal miners have taken caged canaries with them deep into the mines to detect the presence of deadly methane. At the Farts-R-Free Bar & Grill, we received so many citations from the Environmental Protection Agency, we decided to try canaries. But they were just too fragile. At the rate we were killing them off with noxious odors, they would have become an endangered species.

Now we use a herd of filthy emu's brought in from Australia to limit the pollutants emitted from our customer's tail pipes. When the odor level is outrageous, they merely bury their head in the sand, floor boards, or some lady's purse. But if it gets so bad that **they** can't stand the smell, they will attack the offending customer and drive him out into the street. And as smelly as these ol' birds are, you know it's gotta get really bad at times!

These stinky old birds have dramatically reduced our air pollution fines and have reduced the cost of constantly having to steam clean the wallpaper.

PEAS 'N' PORK

Beans ain't the only fuel you can use to power your intestinal cannon. Green peas work very well, too. Thomas Jefferson was supposed to have loved this dish.

green peas ....2 cups
thick sliced bacon .... a slice or two cut up
green onions .... 2 or 3 chopped
parsley, chopped .... about two tablespoons

Cook the bacon slowly in a fry pan to remove as much fat as you can. When the bacon is crisp, remove it to a paper towel and let it cool. Into the fry pan put the other three ingredients and fry about ten minutes. Break up the bacon and add to pan. Fry until the peas are tender. Serve.

It's amazing how such a simple, tasty dish can turn even the most innocent, politically-correct wall flower into a two-legged foghorn who can be heard for miles. Don't wait for a foggy day to try this dish.

Typhoid Mary Wasn't Hated for the Disease She Spread!

She was run out of town on a rail because the flatulence food she prepared destroyed quality of life in her community. They could handle typhoid, but not the stench!

BUNG HOLE BOMBS...

Simple, but effective. Easy to prepare and serve, but the results are unmistakable and inimitable! Next time that security officer at the airport wants to do a full body cavity search on you, you'll be ready for him...

Brussel sprouts .... about a pound
butter .... 2 tbl
flour .... 2 tbl
milk .... milk
dry mustard (not poison mustard gas) .... just a pinch
salt & pepper .... to taste

Dump the peeled sprouts in a pan of salted water and boil fifteen to twenty minutes until tender.

While boiling those bundles of joy, make up a white sauce with the rest of the ingredients. Mix the flour, salt and pepper with the milk. Stir in the melted butter, and dump the whole repulsive-looking mess in a sauce pan. Cook for about five minutes over low to medium heat, stirring, until thickened, or your arm is too tired to continue, or your Margarita needs a refill.

Drain the spouts, cover with white sauce, serve, and listen to everyone complain. When they refuse to eat them, **you** eat all of them, and then in 8 to 24 hours, they will be complaining loud and long about the nauseating fumes drifting toward them from your direction!

Ooooooh! It's SO good....

The dining room is alive with the sound of "music!"

The First Known Fart Cookbook

Historians tell us the first fart cookbook was written by the Transylvanian monk, Smellenk Badt, in 1459. When Gutenberg got wind (literally) of Badt's manuscript he immediately published it. The Bible had to wait.

Rumor has it that Transylvanian, "Vlad, The Impaler", began his reign of terror as an attempt to eliminate everyone using the cookbook because he was so disgusted with the growing air pollution in the mountains. Today, we might call this atrocity "ethnic cleansing". Back then, Vlad, who became known as Dracula, just considered it "atmospheric cleansing."

"FRAGRANT" FRENCH FRIES

Normally we don't use potatoes when beans at hand. But a gigantic portion of fries, catsup, and a stein of beer will have you talking through your butt to a degree never before imagined!

potatoes, red .... two or three pounds
oil (canola or corn oil) .... a couple of quarts

First, find a large pan. For a single serving for one of our typical pants-eater customers we use a 1-1/2 gallon stock pot. You'll need enough oil to fill it to a depth of about 2".

Peel the potatoes. Slice into 3/8" slices in one direction with a chef's knife. Then cut in other direction to get long "fingers" of potatoes.

Important: Spread the fries out on newspapers and let them dry for an hour or so. Excess water will cause dangerous foaming in the hot oil.

Bring the oil up to temperature, about 375°. No higher. A little lower will do. Carefully insert the fries a few at a time until they're all submerged. Fries must float after a minute or two, otherwise those on the bottom will burn.

Don't carelessly dump the whole pile in. You could end up with oil foaming all over the kitchen creating a fire hazard.

Have a fire extinguisher and/or wet towels handy. And DON'T fart while trying this or you could blow the whole kitchen apart!

Stir the fries, keep the temperature near 375°, and fry until golden brown. Remove the fries with a slotted spoon and drain on newspapers. Salt to taste.

Snobs recommend white Idaho potatoes, but that's only because they make nice long fries. Use reds. They're sweeter, brown quicker, and generate far more gas. Sweet potatoes make incredible fries, as well.

Let the oil cool completely, pour through a sieve (to remove particles) back into the bottle, and use the oil again soon. Slightly used oil makes better fries than brand new oil. So for a while each batch of fries will taste better than the last. When the oil finally gets old, mix a little old in with the new.

King Arthur and Sir Lancelot Had an Historic "Falling Out"

Problems first arose between King Arthur and his Knight, Sir Lancelot, not because they both had an intense interest in the queen, but because of the foul gas emitted while the two played the newly invented game of chess.

In fact, King Arthur's round table was made exceptionally large so that no knight would be forced to sit closely to any other knight during the nightly banquet of cabbage and corned beef. The potential for asphyxiation was just too great to take such a chance.

POWER-PACKIN' PEA SOUP

True, peas don't have quite the power of beans, but they come close, and they offer variety to the diet. Studies show you'll have to eat about 36% more to get same detonation power from the same volume of bean soup.

frozen peas	a pound package
chopped green onion	one or two
chicken broth	one can
butter	about a tablespoon
flour	about two tablespoons
milk	two to three cups

Boil the frozen peas in the chicken broth for 10 to 15 minutes until tender. Dump the mess into your blender with part or all of the broth and turn it into a sickening slurry called puree.

While the peas are boiling saute the onion in the butter until tender. Add the flour and milk and cook until thickened – just a couple of minutes.

Add the pureed peas to the onion/milk white sauce. Stir it up. And wolf it down.

Serve with celery sticks, lots of cole slaw, and roasted pecans. Make sure your guests have listed you as beneficiary on their life insurance policy. Check your gas mask cartridge. Get a phony death certificate so that when people complain about the smell you can tell them your grandfather died in the back bedroom a couple of days ago, and you haven't been able to clear the air yet!

Country Club High Jinx

In September 1947, a grudge croquet match between Horgo "The Torch" Buttowski and Billy "The Talking Sphincter" Elliott turned into a sports event that has never been equalled.

Elliott was known for his unethical playing style. Before each croquet match he would gorge himself on beans, cabbage, celery, almonds, brussels sprouts and every type of flatulence food he could obtain. Once in the match, Elliott was known to let rip a noisy, smelly commentary through his stern porthole just as his opponent was about play his ball.

But "The Torch" was also unscrupulous. Just as Buttowski bent over with his mallet, Elliott let go with an explosive fog. Knowing he would, "The Torch" struck his cigarette lighter setting fire to the gas escaping from Elliott and detonating the cloud drifting over the country club.. The croquet courts, the club house, and the forest surrounding were severely damaged by the explosion. And Elliott was last seen streaking into the clouds like the Saturn V moon rocket trailing a mile-long flame.

Horgo "The Torch" Buttowski was awarded the match by default.

ZUCCHINI ZINGERS

Cabbage. Always cabbage. Vital victuals of virulent vapor venters. But a zucchini is a delightfully obscene way to add variety, not to mention stink!

zucchini, shredded .... about a cup
cabbage, shredded .... 2 cups, more or less
green peppers, chopped .... 1/3 to 1/2 cup
pineapple .... almost a cup, or to taste
green onions .... two should do just fine
mayonnaise .... about 1/3 cup
salt, pepper, sawdust, and steel wool .... to taste

Put the shredded zucchini and cabbage in a large bowl, laundry basket, or 55-gallon drum. Chop the pineapple into bite-size pieces so your intoxicated guests don't try to swallow them whole and choke. Mince just the greens from the green onions. After all they are for taste and color. The green will match your guests complexion when you sit this dish in front of them.

Scatter the mayonnaise, salt and fresh-ground pepper over the greens, and toss to coat evenly. Throw in some matchsticks of cucumber to make this salad especially deadly. Or add bits of carrot and tell your guests you don't exactly know what the orange specks are, but that you found them growing among the mold in the mayonnaise and you thought they were so attractive you decided to add them to the salad.

After everyone has left in a panic, you can eat the whole salad yourself and possible end up as an entry in the book of world records.

Beer-Fart Race Car

Dr. Stinko Poopoh, in 1927, designed and built the first race car to be powered by beer farts. Enormous cylinders of highly compressed gas collected from his drinking buddies eliminated the need for gasoline. A secret catalytic converter could oxidize the toxic gas at astounding efficiencies, driving the car to speeds in excess of 200 mph.

Dr. Poopoh hoped to qualify the car in the 1928 Indianapolis 500, but track officials refused to even let him attempt to qualify. They feared that exhaust fumes, being so totally noxious in character, would drive every paying spectator from the stands after the first lap.

In 1973, auto historians took the car out of storage for an illegal high speed run along I-65 from Indianapolis to Chicago. Speeds approaching 140 mph were easily attained. Indiana State Troopers attempting to catch and ticket the driver had to break off the chase and seek medical attention.

The car is now being stored in a secret location.

TOASTED ALMOND BLASTING CAPS

Tasty little morsels, toasted to a rich flavor that, together with a great heavy beer or ale, will put you in the history books as one of the most odorous members of the human race!

almonds .... as many as you can afford, kind of expensive
cumin powder .... plenty
peanut oil .... a couple of tablespoons

Get blanched whole almonds if you can. Otherwise get almonds with the reddish skin and blanch them yourself. Just dump them into a pot of rapidly boiling water for a minute or so, and then put them into cold water to stop the cooking. Blanching makes the skins slide off quite easily. Spread the naked almonds out on a newspaper to dry.

Next, put the dry almonds into a bowl, and drizzle a little oil over them to coat every nut. Spread the slippery little suckers out on a cookie sheet, and sprinkle with lots of cumin powder. Put the cookie sheet into an oven at 350°F for 30 minutes. NO MORE! And you should stir them around about half way through cooking. After toasting, spread them out to cool, and put them in a covered container.

These little critters, when served with other nuts, celery sticks, and a gallon or two of heavy Irish stout will create an intestinal experience that most people experience only once in a lifetime! And your neighbors will pray that it IS only a once in a lifetime event! (If they don't suffer irreversible brain damage before they get a chance to pray...)

PROHIBITED BY LAW

We had intended to reveal some favorite Farts-R-Free Bar & Grill recipes derived from those used by residents of the subcontinent of India to stimulate their tastebuds and their bowels, but we were prohibited, again, by stringent air pollution laws.

Instead, we highly recommend that you refer to a high quality book on Indian Cuisine such as CLASSIC INDIAN COOKING by Julie Sahni, Wm Morrow & Co, 1980. These recipes are top rate (and rate high on the bottom, too) – much too high class for this cheesy (no pun in tended) cookbook.

You MUST try

- **Spicy Potato-stuffed Cabbage Rolls with Ginger Lemon Sauce**

- **Green Peas and Indian cheese in Fragrant Tomato Sauce**

- **Chick-peas in Ginger Sauce**

- **Spicy Brussels Sprouts, Green Beans, and Lentil Stew**

- **Broccoli Smothered in Garlic Oil**

- **Buttered Smothered Cabbage**

- **Glazed Cauliflower with Ginger**

- **Fragrant Buttered Beans**

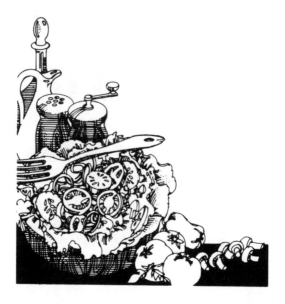

Forget that Useless Nutrition B.S. You're Always Hearing

There is only one rule you must remember about nutrition if you are to eat well: If what you eat gives you gas, it's good for you. If it doesn't give you gas, be suspicious. Your colon will be the final judge.

In other words a thousand farts a day keeps the doctor away. Those who emit toxic vapors will live far longer than those who abstain from one of life's simplest joys.

FRIED WALNUTS

Try this classic Chinese dessert. A five gallon pail of these along with a keg of heavy beer will keep you "exhaling" for months!

walnuts (shelled are easier on the teeth) .... three cups
water, clean .... two cups
sugar .... 1 cup
oil .... enough to do the job

Boil the water, and pour over the walnuts. Let 'em sit for a couple of minutes, and then drain. Put the walnuts in a bowl, sprinkle with the sugar, and mix up. Let them sit for several hours or overnight to dry up.

Put about a cup of peanut oil in a wok (a fry pan will probably be okay) and fry until golden brown. Be careful! These little buzzards are easy to burn. 'Course maybe that's the way you like them.

Remove them from the oil with a slotted spoon and drain on paper towels, or if your neck is really red, just spread 'em out in the bed of your pick up truck to drain. (Careful, the birds will want them.)

Serve 'em hot or cold. When people ask what they are, just tell them you don't know. You just found them lying in the driveway one morning.

Old Navy Diving Suits

Old Navy diving suits like those used to raise the Maine sunk in Havana Cuba in 1898 are now available on various internet auction sites. They can easy be converted into biohazard suits that might not be suitable for modern biochemical warfare, but are more than adequate for use while cooking up the incredible recipes you get here. Instructions for conversion can be found on various internet sites specializing in toxic gourmet cooking.

CHINESE ROASTED PEANUTS

If you ain't heard, it was the Chinese who first developed explosives and fireworks. And judging from their cuisine, they must have had highly developed colonic fireworks, as well!

```
raw peanuts (unroasted, no skins) .................... two pounds
water .............................................. half a cup
salt .............................................. a tablespoon
Five Spice powder ........................................ 1/2 teaspoon
```

You need a good sized roasting pan, or perhaps two. Heat the oven to about 275° or 300°.

While the oven is coming up to temperature, boil the water and mix in the salt and Five Spice powder which is commonly available in grocery stores anymore. Stir in the peanuts. Dump the whole revolting mess into the roasting pan – two if necessary. Spread the peanuts out so they can roast. You don't want a thick layer.

Roast for about an hour, stirring every ten or fifteen minutes, until they are a nice, golden brown.

When cool, put them in a sealed container, and don't share them with anyone. No fartoholic is gonna share his GAStronomical secrets with his buddies.

If the ol' lady complains that you're destroying her kitchen to make food that destroys her air, just pull the cork out of a fine bottle of French Gamay Beaujolais, put a soda straw in it, hand it to her, and tell to "suck this."

DANGER!

"Carvin' the Turkey" While Bathing Can Be Lethal!

Statistics recently released by the U.S. Government show that more 1400 people died last year by drowning in their bathtubs. What most statisticians are too embarrassed to admit is that most of these deaths occurred when the bather was overcome with the toxic fumes of his own making, lost consciousness, slid beneath the surface of the water, and drown.

This is becoming a serious problem! Until now it was thought that taking a bath while making toast was the leading cause of the bathing deaths. Congress considered the problem solved by requiring labels on toasters warning against their use in bath tubs. Unless people taking farting in the tub more seriously, we can only imagine the warning labels Congress will require each of us to wear on our posteriors!

RECTAL ROCKET FUEL

Lentils are potent little beans that might not get you to the moon, but you'll swear there's a trail of fire streaming from your rear end nonetheless! Better get that tub of ice water ready. You'll need to drop your pants and sit in it to put the fire out!

lentils, dry .... 2/3 cup
rice, long brown tastes best .... 1 cup
liquid .... 2 1/3 cup
small carrot 1
celery................................... 1 stalk, more for a faster liftoff
garlic .... 1 clove, smashed
green onion .... a couple, minced

The liquid can be water, but I like to use a cup of homemade chicken stock and 1-1/3 cup of water. Put the liquid in a pot and bring to boil. Add the lentils, rice and all the other goodies and simmer for 45 minutes to an hour. When all the liquid has been absorbed, hit it with a little salt and pepper, and wolf it down. In a mere twenty to twenty-four hours you'll be floating above your favorite easy chair, suspended by a toxic cloud. Put a newspaper on the seat cushion to avoid stains. You'll smell so bad, even the hungriest vulture will be repulsed!

Use this cookbook in good health.
And until we meet again,
here's hoping you
"Keep your bowels open, kid!"